The Lawyer Chronicles

The Lawyer Chronicles

Poems by

Thomas J. Erickson

Cover design by Shay Culligan
Cover art "The Lawyer Chronicles" by Jeffrey Jensen

ISBN: 978-1-952326-52-3

Kelsay Books
502 South 1040 East, A-119
American Fork, Utah, 84003

To my clients. No matter what you did or didn't do.

Acknowledgments

Thanks to the editors of the publications in which the following poems first appeared:

Bramble: "Hot Pot Restaurant No. 9"

New Verse News: "Zoom Court"

Poets Against Hunger (anthology): "Home Visit"

Poetry Midwest: "The Lawyer Who Died in the Courthouse Bathroom"

Rat's Ass Review: "Discovery," "Sandpapering the Witness"

SNR Review: "The Nuptial Flight"

The Legal Studies Forum: "Between Witnesses," "Court Appearances," "Reasonable Doubt," "Word"

The Line-Up, Poems on Crime: "The Breathing Lesson"

The Quiddity International Literary Journal: "The Mother"

The Wisconsin Fellowship of Poets 2013 Calendar: "New Year's Eve 2011"

Verse Virtual: "Blue," "Last Call," "St. Augustine," "The Floating Man," "The Prison Visit"

Verse Wisconsin: "The Killers"

Wisconsin Academy Review: "Chester's Pants"

Word Riot: "Speaking in Tongues"

Contents

The Sentence

On this day in early August, I am on the 4th floor
of the New Deal era courthouse. My black client
is getting sentenced under the Len Bias law for selling
heroin to a white suburban kid who overdosed and died.
There is a mural entitled "Mercy," painted in broad pastels
towering over the judge. Justice cooling a fiery sword
in a trough of water while leaning on her anvil.

I try the best I can: my client is being held criminally liable
because someone else made the voluntary decision to shoot
the drug into his arm; my client had no intention of killing
anyone; he was raised by his mother, who was a crack addict
while his father was in prison; his economic opportunities
as an African-American male in this city were limited
so he turned to selling drugs…

The judge is not having it. As he prattles on about the need
for a twenty-year sentence in his simper and sanctimony,
I stare at the mural, and now I can, at least briefly, go anywhere.

Our lives are an accumulation of duties.
It's in the gaps in between, the intervals,

where the poems begin.

Blue

I leave my white town,
to drive to the black crime
scene in the black neighborhood
where my black client maybe
shot the black girl on the porch
of the house where the blood
stain has turned black.

I take notes in my white
notebook amid the white
noise of the radios and insects
and passing cars and then on
to my office in the white
Third Ward with the white
bars and white restaurants
where I talk to my white
friends about the black men
who played basketball
in front of the white
crowd last night on tv.

Later, I go to the jail and
pass by the white jailers
to talk to my black client
about the charge of the black
on black crime brought by
the white DA before we go
in front of the white judge
and eventually the white
jurors who live in their white
enclaves leading their white
lives and afterward I'll
talk to his black family
about the time he will serve

in the black prison up north
with the white prison guards

and then I'll drive home
past the white park to my house
in the white part of town
and relax and listen to the black
saxophonist who will turn
me blue for a while before
I go to bed to dream my
colorless dreams.

Chester's Pants

Chester kidnapped a woman
outside of a Burger King.

Then he robbed her,
then he raped her,
then he beat her up,
or so they said.

Chester didn't have any
nice clothes for the trial.
When he was arrested,
he was wearing cut-off jeans
and a tank top.
I gave him a shirt and
a pair of pants.

My clothes looked good on him,
especially the pants.
He looked good
when I was sitting next to him
and the jury found him guilty.
He looked good
when I was sitting next to him
and the judge sentenced him to 180 years.

My wife told me
to throw the clothes away.
I did throw away the shirt.
I put the pants in a shopping bag
and put the bag in
a filing cabinet at work.

Years passed,
until today,
when I found the bag.
I put my pants on.
They still fit.
After all,
they are my pants.

The Mother

Informers inform
Burglars burgle
Murderers murder
Lovers love.
—Jean-Paul Belmondo in *Breathless*

My court-appointed client has the scattered
bug-eyed look of a crackhead. Her matted hair
is flecked with platelets of dandruff. She is
wearing a light windbreaker on this cold winter day.

She clutches her keys with both hands
and tells me to help her get her kids back.
She admits she molested her four-year-old son.
Since starting therapy, her thoughts
of having sex with children
are not happening so much.

She shows me a picture of her son
and tells me he can already recite the alphabet.
I mention my sons, and we chat about little things
that make us proud or make us laugh.

Hours later, I drive out of the parking lot.
There she is—hugging herself at the bus stop
in the falling snow.

Home Visit

Oh, but it is buggy
in this upper flat.
The smell of grease,
grease permeating—
Stop cooking those burgers!

Grandmother is wearing a muumuu
of sorts. The holes for her arms
are the size of discuses and show black
muffs of armpit hair. Her grandson wanders in
all bug-eyed and cracked up. He looks
at me askance. He looks askance.

Do they ever turn off the big screen TV?
There is a parakeet or a canary or some such
bird in a white-trimmed cage with a little
sandy colored perch. She is mentally
filliping me. Flick, flick, flick.

Some photos line the wall and provide
the only note of intimacy. How long has
it been since anyone looked into the eyes
of the young newly-weds in their boffo pastels
and bright smiles? There is a sepia one too
of a grand couple in formal wear
which must have been taken
before the diaspora north.

And a three-year-old girl here who is
my ward. Yes, I have wards who form
one of the precincts of my
gerrymandered mind.

She takes me by the hand and leads me
to her bedroom with her Lion King
bedspread and bare walls and silver
radiator blaring unreal warmth.

If not this family for her, who?

Somebody has to hang the pictures,
somebody has to pay the cable bill,
somebody has to hear
the bird sing.

Sandpapering the Witness

Anthony told the detectives that he didn't have sex
with his girlfriend that night, and she was lying
about the assault. A week before the trial, I got a report
that his DNA was found on her vaginal swab, so we had
a problem. Anthony's first reaction was there was no way
that could be true because he knew she took a shower.

I told him he wasn't OJ and I wasn't Johnny Cochran
and there was no way the jury was going to believe
he didn't have sex with her.

Fine, he said, we did have sex, but she consented
and we have sex all the time.

Okay, but why did you lie to the police about it?
I don't know.

You knew she took a shower, right? Yes.

So that's why you lied? Yes.

How were you feeling when the detectives told you
she said you raped her? I was scared.

Why were you so scared? Because last year she lied
to the police about me beating her up, and they believed her.

So, you're going to testify that you lied because you knew she took a shower. If she hadn't taken a shower you would have told the truth, but you were scared because she's a good liar. And you would have no reason to assault her because she was your girlfriend.

Yes, that's right.

Now we're ready for trial.

Zoom Court

It's confounding having a hearing while I'm sitting
in my living room. I have a pandemic beard
and unruly bangs and am wearing boxer shorts
while I position the camera just so to catch
my face and my coat and tie.

Within reach are framed photographs,
books I have loved on the bookcase,
my poetry journals.

My client is on video from the jail. A young
black guy wearing a white mask that gleams
out of the grain. The symbolism is so heavy
it makes me want to reach for my pen.

The Phone

I read on my phone there's a new TV channel just for dogs
and that the weather is going be crummy for my son's prom
tonight. I read on my phone the court petition stating my teenaged
client helped Smokey move the dead girl from the bathtub to the
crawlspace and that the Brewers are losing to the Cards 3 to 1 in
the fifth. I read that Apple sold 74.5 million of these things last
quarter and that 62% of workers at the Fox-Conn factory in
southern China work more than 60 hours/week, making I-Phones.

I read on my phone this quote from Beckett: *Habit substitutes the
boredom of living for the suffering of being* and that we hit two
home runs to tie the game and that Apple made a profit of $13
billion last year and my son will be home from prom at about 4 this
morning and the baseball is traveling farther because of global
warming and that Smokey grabbed a kitchen knife and stabbed her
once in her throat and then in her eye to finish her off and that my
client took her earrings and bracelet and threw them in the trash
and the I-Phones are made with "conflict minerals" that come from
areas engaged in warfare and Fox-Conn is proud to provide a
swimming pool for its workers.

I read on my phone the average Fox-Conn worker makes 200
£/month and that 200 British £ equals $411 and that at least a
dozen workers have jumped to their death in the last three months
and that "billet-doux" is French for love letter and that she might
still have been breathing once they got her to the crawlspace and
that the twelve people who killed themselves were between 19 and
24 years old and that my son has his room assignment for his first
year of college.

I read on my phone anti-suicide nets have been erected to cover 1.5
million square meters at the Fox-Conn factory and that my client is
looking at ten years in prison and that we lost and that tomorrow's
high will be 77 and the low 61 and that maybe it will rain
but I won't know that until tomorrow.

Speaking in Tongues

I smoked a blunt and drank too much bumpy
face so I called a johnny cab to take me to my baby
mama's crib. I saw a brother kickin' it. He said
he got a couchy-coupon from my lady. I said
do you know what time it is and he said it's time
for some drama so I took out my strap
and busted a cap on his ass.

These words—in their doomed vibrancy—literally
mean: I smoked a marijuana and cocaine-laced cigar and
drank too much Seagram's Gin. I called an anonymous
phone number and told them where I was. A few minutes
later, a car picked me up and I gave the driver five dollars.
I told him to drive me to the mother of my child's house.
I saw a guy on the corner who told me that my girlfriend
had propositioned him for sex. I challenged him to a duel
and he accepted. I pulled out my gun and I killed him.

Eventually, I will argue to the jury the following:
My client had a drink with friends. He called a taxi
to take him home to his family. On the way home,
he encountered a long-time enemy of his who spoke
rudely about my client's girlfriend. The man pulled
a gun on my client. My client killed him in self-defense.

I explicate, obfuscate, mitigate, equivocate—
the translator of a story of death.

Word

Interpretation is the revenge of the intellect upon art.
—Susan Sontag

I walk into a video store and ask the clerk
if they have *"I'm Not There."* The clerk
checks his computer and says, *"No
but we have 'I'm Not Scared.'"* His tone
is expectant and hopeful, and it makes me feel
bad to tell him that while it sounds close,
it's not the movie I wanted.

I represent drug clients with the given first
names of *"Kilo"* and *"Easy Money,"* who sell
"teenagers" (one-eighth grams of heroin) to
teenagers. I have two teenagers.

Until a few years ago, I thought the term *"fitful
sleep"* meant a good night's sleep. Now, that I know
the true meaning, I'm not sleeping so well.

HIDTA (pronounced *high-da)* is an acronym
for *High-Intensity Drug Trafficking Areas*
which is an anti-crime task force. My client keeps
complaining that Al Queda is after him.
I think he means HIDTA.

When Kafka read *The Trial* to his friends
for the first time, he laughed so hard
that there were moments when he couldn't
read further. I, for one, do not think
the alienation of modern man is so funny.

Presumption of Innocence

Sometimes it's the big things
that get my clients in trouble:
the fingerprint on the gun,
the surveillance video of the hand-to-hand,
the semen on the bedspread.

Sometimes it's the small things:
a strand of hair on a sweater,
an undeleted Facebook post,
a teardrop tattoo.

I like when the judge tells the jury
If you can reconcile the evidence upon any
reasonable hypothesis other than guilt
then you should find the Defendant not guilty
because it always makes me feel
like we, you and I (not me and some
anxious client) have a chance.

Sure, my fingerprints are everywhere,
not hearing you is part of my DNA,
and that tear in your eye falls too often.

But in the morning, I'll wake up
and take the dog for a walk,
get ready for work, bring you
your coffee, and kiss you good-bye.
You'll smile at me and we'll start the day.

Reasonable Doubt

Once when I was typing an email
my fingers were mispositioned one tab
to the left so when I typed "for" it read "die."
It was a mistake, really. It could have
happened to anyone.

On my I-Phone, my texts of the secret
ingredient read vaginal extract instead
of vanilla extract, and yes, it's my Prius
I'm selling on Craigslist, not my penis.
Damn you, Auto-Correct!

I like telling the jury that if you put
a cat and a mouse in a box and the mouse
disappears, the cat is guilty of murder.
Unless there is a hole in the box.

And that every word that snitch said
was a lie including *and* and *the.* Then
I quote Mark Twain who said, *A lie
can travel halfway around the world
before the truth puts its boots on* before
I implore the jury to put their boots on
and get to work.

And if the verdict comes back guilty, I tell
my client you've got good issues to appeal
and that the judge will temper justice
with mercy when he sentences
you and I won't forget you, I promise.

Burden of Proof

A crack addict client kidnapped
a UWM student and drove her around
and held a gun to her head and raped her
and put her in the trunk of his car and
showed her to his friends and then let her
go at a gas station.

That's what she said he did.

He said he picked her up at a bar
on Brady Street and she wanted
to get high so he bought crack
with her money and she was ready
so he busted his nut in the backseat
and then kicked her out of his car
because it was almost morning
and he was tired and she was getting
to be a clingy white bitch
which bugged the shit out of him.

I don't know what really happened
and I don't care.

Well, it's not like I don't care,
it's that I can't care. It shouldn't make
a difference to me if he did it or not.
It shouldn't make a difference
that my son goes to UWM
and that girl could have been his friend.
It shouldn't make a difference that I get
a palpable thrill when I cross-
examine this girl on the stand.

But what if my doubts are reasonable
and my client did do it?

Then I can tell you I represent evil.
And I can tell you that addiction makes
experience matter. And on we go.

Court Appearances

Where is the poetry in this
boxy room with sallow walls and
carpeting the color of sludge?

Have any of you—judge, DA, bailiff—
ever read the darkly lyrical Larkin while
a client was being deposed or tried
to write a villanelle between appearances?

What if I told you to go
easy on the burglar because even
a flat-screen HDTV doesn't have
the brilliant color of Sonnet #18
or the resolution of any poem
by Frederic Seidel?

Or that the only difference between
the serial arsonist and us is that
he cannot control the terrible freedom
of his thoughts. Isn't there beauty in fire?

The identity thief simply committed
the conceit of the probing author—
to be someone else in secret,
to create a doppelganger. The secret
sharer of Highsmith or Conrad or Twain.

If a line is a point set in motion
then how could the forger stop
once he entered the decimal point?
It was an unbroken line to obfuscation
and abnegation, larceny and lucre.

Maybe the murderer should be set
free because we are all possibly dead
already. I will recite, Judge, to
the hereafter, and if no one comes,
let him go.

The Nuptial Flight

Ninety-nine percent of all the billions of ants
in the world are female. All the ants you see
on the sidewalk or in your garden or in your
kitchen are female. You may never ever see
a male ant in your entire life (unless you dig
up an ant colony—which I have done, by
the way.) The female ants do all the work.
They collect the food, build the nest, defend
the colony, tend to the larvae. The sole task
of the male ant is to inseminate the queen.
When she arrives from her nuptial flight,
the queen chooses a few of the six-legged
bags of sperm. After making their deposit,
they die. When winter comes, the remaining
virgin boys are eaten by their industrious sisters.
These things happen because it is their nature.

On the steps of the courthouse, I
congratulate my client on her divorce
and refer to her by her new last name.
While she asks me out for a celebratory
drink, underfoot, the female ants scurry
about the sidewalk, the indolent males
await their queen in languid repose, and
the queen begins her nuptial flight.

Discovery

In criminal law: Process by which defendant's attorney is given information by prosecution regarding evidence supporting the charges against his client.

Case #1

Cuz brought the two little boys up from Mississippi.
Mom was supposed to come once they got settled
but she stopped answering their calls.

After Cuz's boyfriend was arrested, they moved in with Solei.

Cuz tied up the boys so they wouldn't run away. Solei burned
them with cigarettes and beat them with a belt. No one fed them.
Cuz heard voices and loved to sing them to sleep.

The younger boy stopped breathing so Cuz took them to the
hospital.

The one who lived told the police he loved Cuz.

Case #2

Sometime after midnight, they dragged the rapper to the basement
and choked him to death with a chain because he stole some weed.
They burned the body in a dumpster. A garbage truck dumped
the body in a landfill off Highway 45.

The rapper's blood was found in the basement.
His DNA came back as female.

No one knew but his parents.

Case #3

His wife and kids barricaded the backdoor with a plastic picnic
table, a garbage can, and a grocery cart found off the street
but he busted through and poured gasoline around the kitchen
and living room and lit a match.

He stopped at a gas station to call 911but there was no payphone.
A guy who loaned him his cell phone recognized him from when
they were in jail.

Two of the kids didn't make it out of the upstairs bedroom.
The boy was found draped over his little sister.

The Killers

The killers come and go.
The victims (the alleged victims)
blend together. Almost always
black males either in or on
the periphery of drug dealing.

I write my client's name
on the file in black marker,
read the complaint, go to the jail,
look over the police reports, try
to get him out on bail,
plea bargain or go to trial.
At a sentencing,
the victim's family crying
the same things over and over—
He is missed. He was loved. He loved.

The killers come and go.
So do the rapists,
the armed robbers, and the burglars.
But the child molesters.
I remember them all.
How they look
into my eyes out of some dark
animal terror; how the creepy
fidgeting accompanies every lie;
how the reverie of their terrible
pleasures turns a scowl
into a smile on a dime.

How the steel doors, the electric
locks, the barbed wire
hold us,
bind us.

The Good Laugh

Are you ready for some drama?
That's what the shooter said right before
he shot the man dead at point-blank range.

Six young black males are led into the line-up
room. Once unshackled, they relax and murmur
to each other. The suspect is sixth of six in line.
He doesn't make a peep.

They put on the white jumpsuits
that are puffy and ill-fitting and ride up
at the neck. Once the prisoners notice
how they look they start giggling.

The witness joins the detectives behind
the one-way window. Number One takes
his mark, steps forward, and flatly says,
Are you ready for some drama? Number Two
utters the line with mild defiance. Number Three,
with no prompting, lurches toward the glass
and commands, *You ready for some drama, bitch!*
The boys start laughing uncontrollably.
Once order is restored, Four and Five proceed
without incident. Then, it's Number Six's turn,
his voice barely audible.

The witness marks the card.
The boys are led out of the room.
The chains scuff the tile floor.

The Breathing Lesson

The pock-marked Formica,
the gouged and graffitied table,
the walls the color of piss,
into the cell, comes Nakia.

I catch my breath—not at the sight
of the gaunt young black woman
in her gleaming shackles and maroon jumpsuit—
but at her smell. It is a biting
stench of sweat and shit and urine.
A sirocco that fills the room
with a primordial odor of life and death.

Nakia tells me that while she was
in the back seat, the other girl
was in the front giving head to the john.
The drip of cocaine fell
from Nakia's nasal passage to the back
of her throat. She swallowed hard
and pulled the trigger.
One shot to the back of his skull.

Gary Gilmore told Mailer that the reason
he wanted to die was because of the noise.
Now, as I ask Nakia about her life,
we are drowning in electronic door slams,
shouted expletives, scraping footsteps,
and the white noise of transistor radios.

She draws me in with her history
of mother's beatings and
uncles' molestations and her abortion
at fourteen. I ask her something I never ask:
why did you do it?

She was killing to bring back her lost
children, clean her poisoned blood,
clear her drug-addled mind. She was
gasping for one last breath of air
and now I would be her final accomplice.

The Floating Man

Tonight I am in a mist. I barely know what's what.
                                —John Keats

It started during a trial. I was sitting there listening
to the DA's opening statement when I started
floating about the courtroom,

over the judge, the jurors, the bailiffs, my client,
the victim's family wearing matching shirts
with his super-imposed photo.

I could even see me—whispering to my client,
taking notes, staring into space. I looked tired
and I needed a haircut.

The next time I floated, I was at a baseball game
with my two sons. They were still pretty little.
I let them climb

to the top row of the upper deck. I drifted way up to
keep an eye on them.

Far above the stadium, I could see the arc of the fly
ball that fell to the glove of the outfielder
with such regret,

I would have kept going if they hadn't pulled me
down.

The Prison Visit

Because I'm an attorney and know where I'm going, I don't
need an escort to walk to the infirmary to see my guy
once I pass through security at the gatehouse.

A couple of inmates come up the path dressed in dark green.
Neither is one of my old clients but you never know. We don't
make eye contact but our shadows touch as we pass.

I am visiting Paul. He is paralyzed from the waist down and
partially blind after being shot by the cops. He has a little goatee,
which another inmate has to shave. He's been in for twenty years
and will die before he makes parole. I don't want to lie so I don't
bring it up.

He spends his days listening to music and lying in bed. He tells me
he's lucky because his room in the infirmary has a window.
He can't see much of anything but the light is different and
sometimes in the morning, the sun touches his face. He's begun
listening to classical music and really likes Vivaldi.

On the walk back to the gatehouse, I realize I probably won't see
Paul again. It's kind of a relief because I can't do anything for him
anyway. Plus, no one's paying me anymore. He'll die in his room
someday. His earphones will be in, and no one will hear the
symphony.

New Year's Eve, Milwaukee, 2011

I only go out to get a fresh appetite
for being alone. That was Byron,
I only go out to get the bag
on. That was me.

Down to the dingy bar I go. Say goodbye
Catullus to the shores of Asia Minor. Say
goodbye Tom to the curbs of Whitefish Bay.

My favorite color is Glenlivet brown and tonight
I'm going to prove it.

I hope I see Jimmy but he's probably making
popcorn for the crowd at the Globetrotters' game.
I'd like to play cribbage with Mike but he's dead.
At least, Ted the heroin addict bartender is
here but so is that shrew whose husband
I represented in the divorce. Good God.

The sound of the bar dice is an anodyne.
Shots all around. All of us in this musty boat
must imagine Sisyphus happy. If not,
how could we cut the deal, how could we
bring 'em back, how could we avoid
the skunk?

This is New Year's Eve in Milwaukee
for fuck's sake.

Last Call

Of course, no one believes we hit 40 bars in one night.
But yes, children, we did, in an endless summer night
in the timeless burg known as Sheboygan, Wisconsin,
the Year of our Lord Ronald Reagan, 1981.

It was me and Greg and Dave and Al and Scott and
we started at 6 o'clock on a Friday night.
Dave was driving his dad's car.

These were the last of the halcyon days of Sheboygan
bars when there was still a bar on every corner and
the drinking age was a blessed 18 and if you took
the "U"—Indiana to Eighth Street to Michigan,
there was a domino row of taverns, tippling one
into the other with a beautiful hazy momentum.

The rules were one tap beer (Pabst or Kingsbury or Miller)
(usually eight to twelve ounces) (if you do the math,
by the end of the night, that's at least 400 ounces
of beer—the equivalent of 33 bottles of beer for each of us)
(which isn't really all that much in eight hours for a kid
who was 20 years old in Sheboygan County where
and when beer ruled the world) (the taps were anywhere
from 25 cents to 40 cents, so we spent about $15 each
which wasn't too bad because I was making $3.35 an hour
picking up garbage) (although the cheapest was 15 cents
at the 1136 Tap) and various other rules depending on
our whims per bar: slam; no one talks; pinky extended;
parlez-vous Francais?

Andy's Bar, Ziggy's, Head East, The 1136 Tap,
Four of a Kind, Pool Tap, The Blue Room, The Tipo (where
one of the denizens uttered "The Mod Squad's here" when
we rolled in), *The 99 Club, Harbor Lights, the K and R Saloon,*

Cecil's Palace, Mr. Glen's, Dick Suscha's Coho Bar, Who's Inn,
and so many more sunk these days by drunk driving laws
and/or the allure of drinking at home watching Netflix
or naughty things on the internet.

Later, we bragged of our exploits. If you knew us back
then you would have believed it because it was well
established that Al and I had drunk a quarter- barrel
by ourselves and the other guys were no weak-tits either.

And why not brag? At least we were good at something.
We were all heroes that moment at bar time when
we were staggered and weak-kneed
and somehow still standing.

Before the marriages
and the kids
and the jobs.

Before we pressed on.

Before we had to be okay.

St. Augustine

Everything is the oldest here—
the oldest house, the oldest mission,
the oldest park where they walk past
the bromeliads and seashell geegaws
for sale on the site of the oldest slave market
in North America.

There are firsts here too—
the first fort, the first Catholic
mass, the first permanent outpost
of European civilization, the first infliction
of the white man's burden.

The man and woman are getting older
and neither of them are firsts.

She swims in the waves in her peacock
colored swimsuit; he tries to body surf
on a boogie board but ends up
looking for seashells.

At night, the terrace door is open
the dreams come in increments.

For him, it's Martin Luther King and JB Stoner
and Woolworth's lunch counters and beaches
in this oldest and first and most segregated town.
Then the dreams go back even further,
to the first slaves, the Fountain of Youth,
the blood on the beach.

For her, it's the water and living things
under the water and how she wants to go
there and hide from this heavy, plain
history and fold herself forever
into the lullaby of the surf.

Hot Pot Restaurant No. 9

There's a video of a baby rat being pulled by chopsticks out of a hot pot at a chain restaurant in China. The woman on the other side of the table reading an article on her Kindle is agog. The article is about scientists giving Ecstasy to octopi to see if it makes them less antisocial.

Years ago, I saw the moon set like the sun one black night and then come right back up like a yo-yo. I asked the twin wood sprites, Oswaldo and Hidalgo, who I was. They fiddled on their abaci and said, with their impish grins, "You are the sum of your regrets."

I have a client in Ojai who's facing federal prison for mortgage fraud. She's got PTSD from her kids ODing, but she's relieved her new therapist says that her old therapy of "more truth equals more healing equals more reconciliation" is nothing less than the awful tyranny of total recall. She's learning how to *remember to forget*

which would be good advice for more than just the shocked diners at Hot Pot Restaurant No. 9.

Foundations 2020

Any line of questioning needs a foundation to be relevant in a courtroom. If you're on trial for murder, I'm not supposed to ask you what you made for breakfast unless you're on trial for killing someone by poisoning the scrambled eggs, for example.

Nonetheless, I have asked several objectionable questions in my life, whether in the courtroom:

Did you stop that car because a black guy was driving?

How much is the State paying you to say that?

How do you sleep at night?

or outside a courtroom:

Are you sure you're pregnant?

Is that what you're wearing?

Didn't you stop drinking?

Now my questions have a more troubling foundation, and they are not meant to provoke or to play. I ask them to myself, mostly.

How did we get here?

Where are we going?

Will we be okay?

How do any of us sleep at night?

The Lawyer and the Thief

I never see anyone I know anymore
at Summerfest, like the time I was pissing
in the trash can in a jammed men's room
when the guy across from me looked up
and said, "Hey man, aren't you my lawyer?"
Indeed, 'twas Carlos, an inveterate burglar
client of mine.

Several months later, Carlos and I are sitting
safely in a dismal courtroom in a dismal
building called the Safety Building. He's about
to get a couple of years in prison and we have
a few moments to relax before the judge takes
the bench. Carlos tells me it's really not so bad
in there. "I don't have to make any decisions
and I can just sit there and think." "Yeah,"
I say, "that's pretty cool, I think."

It's almost noon by the time court is finished.
I drive back to my office on a sunny day
in late October. My mental clock is racing:
court appearances, my children's obligations,
deadlines for this and that…

Carlos already evaporating.

Prelude to Sleep (or What I Often Think About When Lying in Bed)

Canoodling with my wife
but she's just about out and the dog's between us
and do I really want to disturb him?

How many games the Brewers are out of first place.
Jim Bouton said you spend your whole life
gripping a baseball and it turns out it was
gripping you all along.

My court case tomorrow.
The judge will blame my Mexican client
for bringing heroin into the country
and I will argue people take drugs when
they are hurting. There is something wrong
with the soul of America and he was just
trying to kill our collective pain.
Yeah, it would be cool to say that…

And lastly, what poem I'll work on next.

Then, going to sleep is like a low camber
on a sharp curve.

The wheel of imagination turns best in the dark.

In an Empty Courtroom

To my surprise, no one's around.
The bailiffs are getting the prisoner
from the jail; the clerk's in the back
somewhere; the judge still at lunch.

The defense table is skirted with heavy black cloth
to prevent the jury from seeing
the defendant shackled to the iron rings
cemented to the floor.

The clerk's station is adorned
with a few withering plants. On the wall
is a portrait of a long-dead judge gazing down
on me with bored benevolence.

I run my hand the length of the polished wood
in front of the jury box. Looking up,
I can see the scattershot of dead bugs
in the big light fixtures suspended
like dim globes about to fall.

I take the witness stand and look out
at the empty gallery and wonder what
to say or whom to answer. I wonder too
about the time I have spent in this room
and the representations I have made—
of my clients and of myself.

Someday, surely, this courtroom will shutter,
this place of deliberation and whim,
of bondage or freedom. A shell
and a citadel. And now, a place, for me,
of a sudden discordant contentment.

Who will be the very last
to be judged here?

What did he do?
What did they say he did?

Who will be me?

The Lawyer Who Died in the Courthouse Bathroom

As a young man, he read Camus and resolved
that if God did exist it wouldn't make any difference.

He went to Spain and almost didn't come back.

Once, he snow-shoed eight miles. There wasn't
a sound in the woods that day, not even birdsong.
Just the snowshoes breaking through the icy
crust to the powder—and his misty breath in
and out. He walked across a frozen pond
where he hunted for turtles when he was a kid.
They were hibernating in the frosty ooze below.

The hundreds of people he represented;
their dramas not worth one whit.
The files waiting in his briefcase,
the combination set to open.

About the Author

Thomas J. Erickson is a poet and attorney in Milwaukee, Wisconsin, where he sometimes works on his poems while sitting in court waiting for his cases to be called. A Pushcart Prize nominee, he has published two chapbooks and one collection called *The Biology of Consciousness* (Pebblebrook Press). His poems have been published in numerous journals and anthologies. He is a proud member of the Hartford Avenue Poets.